THE INFINITE POWER OF YOU

22 Secrets to Discovering Your Power!

Nanice Ellis

WWW.NANICE.COM

Special Create Space Edition
ISBN: 978-1511476362

Edited by Tom Cantrell

Interior and Cover Designed By

ecko
PUBLISHING
WWW.ECKOPUBLISHING.COM

*To my children Dustin, April, Travis and Clay
who constantly teach me more than
I could ever teach them.*

Nanice Ellis

If you knew you had a million dollars buried in your backyard, would you just leave it there? Or, would you dig it up and become an instant millionaire? Your Infinite Power is your fortune buried inside you. No one can dig it up for you. No one can steal it from you. You and only you have 100% of the rights to your fortune. Whether or not you choose to uncover it, it is yours eternally and unconditionally.

Nanice Ellis

Table of Contents

Chapter 13

Chapter 14

Chapter 15

Chapter 16

Chapter 17

Chapter 18

Chapter 19

Chapter 20

Chapter 21

Chapter 22

The Infinite Power Of You!
Nanice Ellis

Did you know that you are as perfect and powerful as any being who has ever lived? Of all the great and powerful souls who have walked this planet, Buddha, Christ, Mohammed, Mother Theresa, Gandhi, Socrates, Confucius, not one of them is any more or less powerful than you. You are infinitely and intrinsically perfect and powerful. Right now. Without conditions.

If we are all intrinsically and inherently perfect and powerful, we cannot then ever be imperfect or not powerful. It is impossible to give up something that is intrinsic or inherent. It also means that you cannot be more or less perfect or powerful than anyone else and you need do nothing to become a powerful being. You already are. You may not remember your power or even have faith in it. In this moment, you may feel scattered and defocused - and therefore diminished – but your power is still with you - in you and through you. All you have to do to live powerfully and successfully right now is recognize, reclaim and refocus that which is already yours; your inherent and intrinsic personal power, the birthright of a perfect soul.

If all beings are equally powerful, why do we show up expressing comparatively different levels of power? Why do some of us appear less powerful? Or feel less perfect than others? Is it is because we forget that we really are powerful and simply don't express it? Or perhaps it is because we divert our power, misdirect it, scatter or diffuse it?

At sixteen years old, I suffered terribly at the hands of an abusive boyfriend. I was thrown out of a moving car, pushed through a glass shower door, strangled, suffocated – severely battered in so many ways. I experienced excruciating, emotional, mental, and spiritual pain. I constantly felt weak and powerless – victimized by the whims and desires of someone who seemed much more powerful than I. If you had told me then that I was all powerful, I would have thought you were crazy. I was unaware of who I really was. Looking at my life through my interpretation and imagination (my filters), I assumed I was powerless and, therefore, I appeared so to myself and the world – particularly to those who would take advantage of my vulnerability.

The more powerless I felt – the more powerless I believed myself to be – the more powerless my experience "proved" me to be. I did a great job playing the part of the powerless victim of circumstance. Each time I was beaten up physically, verbally or emotionally I more deeply suppressed any knowing or remembrance of my power, especially the power to walk away from abuse and degradation.

When things were looking the worst, I believed I would simply die at the hands of my abuser – the person I thought I loved and wanted most to love me. But somehow I retained a spark of self esteem kept deep within me like a coal buried in dark ashes. Through all the beatings and abuse, this bit of remembrance of who I really am stayed safely hidden until one day, that buried seed of remembrance sprouted just enough to give me the courage I needed to leave - once and for all.

It took me many years to realize that even at my lowest most terrifying moment – even as I thought I would be killed and was struggling for my last breath, I was no less powerful than the most powerful person in the world. If I had for one moment remembered my inherent perfection and power, what would have been possible for me? If I knew I was intrinsically powerful, would it have been even possible to allow myself to continue suffering abuse, confusion, isolation? Would I have remained, stuck, desperately depressed and even passively suicidal?

You might not be suffering at the hands of an abuser, as I was, but how might you be keeping yourself powerless? Are you at a job which doesn't support you? Are you disrespected by friends or relatives? Are you hiding gifts and talents out of fear of failure? Are you not speaking your truth because you fear certain consequences? Are you in a relationship that limits your ability to express who you really are? Are you not doing what you really want to do because you lack the confidence to do so? How are you keeping yourself powerless?

Now, wait. This is not the time to beat yourself up by feeling bad about your choices; but it is the time to remember that powerlessness does not suit you. It never has and it never will. It is time to realize that you are perfect and powerful right now – and there is absolutely nothing you need to do to prove it. It is time to remember and embrace the power of who you really are. It is simple – maybe not easy – but I know you can do it.

Imagine for a moment that you are, right now perfect in every detail; physically, mentally, spiritually. Imagine also that you are all powerful and that nothing is impossible for you.

If you knew you possessed infinite and intrinsic power right now, who would you be? What would you do?

Let the journey begin…..

Nanice Ellis

I am perfect and powerful right now

Who are you? Who are you really? Are you defined by what you own? By what people think of you? Are you your job title? Your possessions? Your relationships? The content of your life? What if you were defined by none of these things? What if you were truly an infinitely powerful being and the trance of materialism has led you to temporarily forget your inherent value and personal power?

This is your wake up call.

Make a list of everything which you feel defines who you are; your roles, your relationships, your possessions – everything that is really important. Everything that you feel defines who you are to your family and friends; competitors and associates. Got it? Thank you.

Now throw it away. Rip it up and throw it away!

Every thing on that list limits you; especially if you use those things to define who you are.

Are you the CEO of a large company? Are you the president of a powerful country? Even those roles keep you small if you use them to define who you are. If your sense of personal power is dependent on the content of your life, your possessions, relationships and roles, you are on a roller coaster ride – a narrow, one track ride with ups and downs controlled by everyone and every thing – but you!

You have heard it said that "change is the only constant." It's true. If there is anything consistent and predictable about life, it is inconsistency and unpredictability. We can always count on things to change. If our sense of personal worth and power is dependent on the content of our life, we feel powerful only that small percentage of the time when everything is exactly how we want it to be.

What would happen if your sense of power was unconditional and you knew that it was not contingent on anyone or anything outside yourself? What if external circumstance could not affect your sense of who you really are because you knew your intrinsic perfection and personal power was unaffected by the inconsistencies of your human experience?

Nanice Ellis

Pretend for a moment that you are in fact an all powerful being – unaffected by environment or circumstances, uncontrolled by anything outside yourself. How does that look? How do you live your life? How do your relationships change? How do you respond when things don't go according to plan? If you knew you were in fact all powerful right now, who would you be? How would you feel? If you are not acting that way right now, you are reacting to circumstances and not responding to the world as the inherently perfect and powerful being you really are.

You were born a perfect being. You always have been and always will be inherently and intrinsically powerful. You have allowed circumstance to define who you are for way too long. It's time to stop being governed by anything or anyone outside yourself and be who you really are; to acknowledge and own the infinite power of you –respond to life accordingly – and enjoy the benefits that will now come to you naturally and effortlessly.

Nanice Ellis

Chapter 2

I express and act on creative ideas

When I was in the third grade, my class was given an assignment to explore our creative ability by inventing a new toy. I went home, found a box, and made it into an incredible launching machine. I was so excited that I could create such a wonderful and unusual invention. Suddenly, I was afraid to bring it to school. I was afraid that if others rejected my best creation – the best I had to offer – they would be rejecting the best of me – and I would find out I wasn't worthy. I wasn't prepared to be that vulnerable, so to protect my ego I diminished my self and my creation (before someone else had the chance to) by not even taking it to school. Instead, I brought a simple stream of looped paper which did nothing.

When it was my turn to show off my "invention", my disappointed teacher criticized me in front of the class and told everyone that it wasn't any kind of invention at all. She implied I had no creativity. I felt inadequate and shamed. I remember thinking about my incredible launching machine now hidden in my bedroom closet. I regretted that my fear of rejection had made me leave it home.

What I feared, I created by giving in to my fear. I failed to express my self and my creativity and as a result, showed up with less than what I was capable of. My fear of rejection, kept me from expressing who I really was. Consequently, the "lesser me" was rejected and all of me felt it.

What revolutionary, creative, life changing ideas stay buried inside you because you fear rejection? How small do you feel you have to live in order to be safe? Is playing it safe worth the real risk of not living the life you really want?

It is good to be honest with yourself. It is healthy to admit when you are afraid. What is limiting is to give in to your fear without challenging it. Fear's job is to keep you safely in your comfort zone so that you don't do anything to risk your identity; your idea of who you are and have to be in order to be O.K in the world. In most cases, fear does a great job because it keeps us from venturing out and expressing parts of ourselves which might be rejected and therefore threaten our identity. But if fear is in charge of your actions and behaviors in the world, your world will stay limited. Do you want to live a limited and limiting life? Then give in to fear without question or challenge. You may not choose to be afraid, but you certainly can choose whether to give in to fear without a challenge. Here is where you get to decide what the rest of your life will look like.

Choice one: Allow fear to do it's job and keep you safe in a limited world. Choice two: Remember that fear is nothing next to your inherent and infinite power - allow the possibilities of your life to become limitless by uncovering your hidden creativity and sharing it with the world.

Yes, it's possible you might experience the rejection of others - actually it is likely that the more amazing the idea, the more surely you will experience criticism and rejection but is any rejection so great or so damaging as rejecting yourself and not expressing who you really are? When you avoid expressing something because of your fear of rejection, you actually reject your own idea and ultimately yourself. What would happen if you unconditionally accepted yourself and owned your power to create and express your ideas, your beliefs, and who you really are without fear?

Do you want to live a full and joyful life without fear of rejection? You can. Right now. You have everything you need - right now. Joy and happiness isn't anywhere in the future – it is now. You get to experience everything at the end of the rainbow simply by being the rainbow. You are the rainbow when you live every moment expressing your grandest, simplest, and even silliest ideas. We are all full of ingenious creativity and it takes a lot more energy to hold it all in with the gates of fear than to just be ourselves and express all parts of us. Maybe it's your job to be the first on your block or in your cubicle to proclaim yourself to be a magnificent, creative, powerful being. You don't have to stand on your desk or your roof to do this - you simply have to stand up for who you really are and be yourself unconditionally. You can do it - and I can't wait to see the beautiful unique expression of who you really are.

CHAPTER 3

I have the courage to be vulnerable

The strongest people I know can express deep emotion. It generally takes more courage for men to be vulnerable – to reveal deep, sometimes tender feelings and be open to rejection or even ridicule – than to stand up to a physical assault or jump out of a plane. Many men declare confidently that they "say it like it is," yet they have difficulty expressing love for their partner or showing tender feelings to a child.

While it may be more socially acceptable for women to express themselves emotionally, many women also find it difficult to express how they truly feel – especially in a business setting – for fear of showing up as weak and too "emotional" to be trusted with "tough decisions." Consequently, hurt, frustration, even confusion, are held back until they are expressed as anger; while soft and tender feelings simply stay hidden. No one knows how you really feel, so they assume you don't really care.

How easily do you express how you really feel? Are you afraid of your feelings? Are you afraid that if you express them, someone will reject or judge you? Are you then unable to express genuine feelings? Do you instead bottle them up until they are expressed as something else? Do we hide feelings because we believe that if we are feeling something we think we ought not to feel, then we ourselves are lacking or "wrong"? Is it possible that no one is judging you at all? Is it possible that you are judging your own feelings then transferring that judgment to others – thinking they are judging you?

Perhaps you are feeling something you don't approve of. Perhaps you are angry at an irritating spouse, an inconsiderate friend, or an errant son or daughter – and you don't like how you feel. What if you knew that you were not your feelings? Would you be better able to accept them? What if you could de-attach your identity from how you feel and just accept your feelings as simply a barometer of how you are experiencing life in the moment?

If you were able to accept your feelings would you be better able to express them? Let's face it, you, me, and everyone else, has experienced thousands of feelings over our lifetimes. Have any of those feelings ever killed us (if so, you wouldn't be reading this)? Has the expression of those feelings (if spoken before they get so big they become something else) ever really cost us anything significant?

No matter what our feelings, we will survive – and thrive – if we express them. It's OK to feel sad, angry, jealous, frustrated and scared. It is even more OK to express them honestly – especially if you can do that without judging yourself or anyone else.

Having worked with thousands of people all over the world, I've come to learn that we are all pretty much the same on the inside. We all feel joy and pain and have the same or similar emotional needs. Perhaps the reason we think we are so different is because, like us, most everyone else is also afraid to express that part of themselves that feels confused, lost, or vulnerable.

There is nothing you have felt or are feeling now – there is nothing you can express – that a million other people on our planet haven't felt or expressed. You can change your life right now by having the courage to express how you really feel. If you don't know for sure how you feel, express that. Say it like it is when your feelings first come up – before you stuff them back down and they become something they are not.

Perhaps your courage to share the most intimate parts of who you are will open a greater and safer space for others to do the same. When we all communicate how we really feel – honestly and openly – without judging ourselves and others – our world begins to grow and expand to support the greater, more powerful version of who we really are.

CHAPTER 4

I visualize only that which I desire

Do you ever visualize? When I ask this question of my audiences, only a few hands go up. When I ask if anybody ever worries, every hand goes up. What about you? What you may not realize until now is that worry is visualization – negative visualization. You are actually creating a mental image of that which you don't want – and focusing on it – playing the tape in your head until "voila" like magic the very disaster you were imaging comes into reality. In the negative sense, that is exactly how visualization works.

Does this type of mental imaging make you feel powerful or powerless? Every time we focus on a negative outcome, we misdirect our power. We believe and act contrary to the amazing powerful beings we really are. That is why it feels so uncomfortable to hold images of imperfection, problems and failure in our perfect minds. It's true that sometimes things don't seem to go according to plan; but a person who keeps positive focus on what is wanted has a better chance of manifesting and materializing what they really do want than someone stuck in worry over that which they don't want.

It was Christmas eve, 1975. I was twelve years old. Mom and Dad were taking me out for our traditional holiday dinner at a beautiful old restaurant in Great Neck, New York. As we drove up Northern Blvd, my mother quietly announced that she was not able to find the only thing I had on my Christmas list – the only thing I really wanted – a green figure skating skirt. She had looked for one for weeks and "it just didn't exist". I had planned to wear my new skating skirt that week on Christmas vacation. I was convinced that by wearing a green figure skating skirt – just like Dorothy Hammel's, I could figure skate just like she could. It hadn't occurred to me that I had no previous figure skating experience; I just knew I could, if only I had "that" skirt.

Now, I could have imaged a ruined Christmas and focused on a disappointing Christmas vacation, but I could "see" myself in that skirt too clearly – and refused to give up my vision. As we pulled into the restaurant parking lot - there it was! My green skating skirt; displayed in the window of the new sporting goods store right next door to the restaurant. The store had already closed but we tapped on the window and banged on the door insistently until the weary store clerk let us in. Strangely, they didn't seem displeased; in fact I had a feeling that they were expecting me.

The only skating skirt they had was the one in the window – and it was my size! But I wasn't shocked or amazed. My vision was so clear to me; I had imagined no other possibility. The next day my parents took me to a skating rink in the Catskills. I glided onto the ice in my new green skating skirt – I was a figure skater; I skated backwards, did spins and figure eights. It wasn't until someone asked me where I had learned to skate as well as I did, that it occurred to me that I learned to skate in the same place that I created the image of my little green skating skirt – my mind.

You've heard the expression "a mind is a terrible thing to waste" but have you ever been taught to intentionally harness the power of your mind through visualization? What would happen if you started treating your mind as the powerful creator it really is? What if you knew your mind was somehow tied into a higher mind which not only contains every conceivable and inconceivable possibility but also provides everything you need in order for your visualization to manifest in your life?

Are you mastered by your thoughts? Do your worries govern your life? How would your life change if you were the master and your incredible mind was a faithful, powerful, servant who would bring to you everything you desire? All you have to do is decide what you do want and keep the vision clear (sort of like worrying in reverse).

Positive visualization has unlimited power in attracting what we want. When we visualize "failure" we usually feel blocked and confused; but when we focus on success – on the image of what it looks and feels like – we feel successful and confident, emotionally insisting on the results we see in our mind. Amazingly a clear path opens up – sometimes in the most remarkable ways. Maybe there is a "green skating skirt" waiting for you if you have the courage to dream it and accept your inherent right to it.

CHAPTER 5

I possess infinite "soul esteem"

Like most people, you probably take care of yourself just fine. You eat regularly, shower daily, brush your teeth thoroughly – and when you do something noteworthy, maybe you treat yourself to dinner, a movie or reward yourself with a massage.

You take care of yourself physically; but how do you regard yourself? How do you feel about yourself? Do you appreciate yourself or beat yourself up emotionally? Are you your best friend or worst critic? Are you your own cheerleader or do you treat yourself as if you were your own enemy?

If you really want to know how you regard yourself, listen to the way you talk to yourself.

How you talk to yourself directly and immediately affects the quality of your life. When you put yourself down, does it energize or weaken you? Does it inspire or drain you? People who regard themselves highly, those who have healthy self esteem, are happier, live more productive lives, tend to be more highly regarded and socially sought out – and even make more money.

Many of us regard ourselves poorly because our self worth is dependent on external results. If you succeed by society's definition, you feel good about yourself – you regard yourself highly; but if you fail, you believe that you are not worthy of good feelings. You "failed" and therefore aren't as good as someone else – or even as worthy as you were yesterday when you did succeed. If your self worth is dependent on anything outside yourself– I mean any thing – then the way in which you regard yourself will change from day to day and even minute to minute as circumstances change from day to day and minute to minute

What if your self esteem wasn't dependent on anything or anyone? What if you knew you didn't have to prove your worth or live up to any expectations in order to be worthy? What if your sense of self worth was unconditional? Would you react to constantly changing circumstances by constantly shifting your belief in and image of yourself? Or would you stay focused and on target - owning and expressing your power unconditionally?

You are worthy right now just because you are – just for being. Your conditional self esteem is now unconditional "soul esteem". It doesn't change as life changes but remains constant regardless of circumstance - it is as eternal as your soul. When you experience soul esteem, self esteem is guaranteed and you know your worth is unconditional, infinite and eternal.

When you know yourself to be unconditionally worthy, you step into your power. Your confidence and willingness to take intelligent risks goes through the ceiling. You experience "soul esteem". You feel great regardless of external circumstances and every day really is a great day. Others want to be around you; because, as you regard yourself well, you naturally regard others well.

Do you want to know how happy you will be tomorrow? Simply look at how you regard yourself today. No matter what "success" you attain, you will never enjoy it if you regard yourself critically; however, if you regard yourself as inherently and unconditionally valuable and powerful, with infinite and unlimited "soul esteem" you will live the most joyful life possible – no matter what. Your happiness is "soul-ly" conditioned on how you choose to regard yourself – starting right now.

Nanice Ellis

I will not wear someone else's plaid polyester leisure suit!

I grew up in New York in the seventies when hip huggers were hip and beads, braids, and bell bottom jeans were an essential symbol of "cool." Sadly, I was anything but cool.

I was studious, smart and virtually friendless. I also wore plaid polyester leisure suits to school. If the term "nerd" had been coined, I would have worn the label. My very opinionated mother dictated my attire. She was only trying to give me some dignity and protect me from the style of the "godless, tasteless hippies."

By the time I was in junior high, I was pretty much brain-washed to accept my mother's way of dressing. This was truly amazing, considering the daily harassment I received from the other kids. I should mention that they did not make leisure suits in kid's sizes (gee, I wonder why) so my mom bought adult sized suits and did her best to tailor them to "fit" me. Luckily, the jackets hung low enough to mask the low hanging crotch of the over-sized pants. The mixtures of pastel patterns weakly challenged the vibrant colors of the hip generation, the cool kids, the in-crowd. I didn't even have a group to identify with – except the beehive coiffed teachers pushing retirement – this was not the epitome of cool.

I hated those leisure suits. I hated the taunting and teasing – the ostracizing – I got from the in-crowd (and even the out-crowd!) because I wore them; but even more than that, I hated the reaction I believed I would get from my mother if I told her the truth.

We will do almost anything including sacrificing our greatest desires in order to get acceptance, approval, love, understanding, or appreciation. But every time we fail to honestly express our needs or opinions in order to get our emotional needs met, we diminish the expression of our power. I was 12. My mother was important to me. I really wanted to please her – be accepted by her – I tried to express myself as she wanted me to, but it wasn't me I was expressing; and it didn't work.

Finally, the day arrived where I just couldn't take it anymore. I timidly told my mother I wanted to wear bell-bottom jeans like the other kids. She responded by saying, "Why would you want to wear those ugly things?" And immediately bought them for me. Although I never completely conformed to the ways of my peers, I did find the space to explore my own expression of who I believed I was. I loved those jeans. They were dark denim with a rainbow going all the way down the leg. That rainbow led to freedom – a freedom which was evidently much closer to my reality than I had believed. It was not my mother who prevented me from expressing myself, keeping me imprisoned in plaid polyester leisure suits. It was my fear of the consequences; my fear of rejection from the person I loved and needed to be loved by the most that kept me from exploring who I was.

How might you be wearing someone else's plaid polyester leisure suit? Does it fit? Does it express who you are? Why are you wearing it?

- Do you fear rejection or other negative consequences if you express yourself in ways that might not be acceptable to someone else?

- Are you altering your life or sacrificing who you are in order to get your needs met? Approval? Acceptance? Love? Respect?

- Are you adopting others' style and failing to

discover and express your own?

- Are you involved in a religion or other organization which doesn't support your true beliefs?

- Do you keep your mouth shut when your truth is screaming to be heard?

- Do you live in ways that constrict your greatest expression?

- Do you compromise who you are in order to get what you want or to feel a certain way?

The emotional cost of not showing up as our real selves is much more damaging than not gaining acceptance, love or approval. Even if we can manipulate or hide our real selves enough to get our emotional needs met by others, it is not really us they are seeing and we will still feel like we are missing something.

It is OK to dress how you like; think how you please, and speak your truth as you believe it. You will never be successful in getting what you want by sacrificing who you are. When you begin to own your truth and express your own personal "style" whether that is how you think, speak, write, create, or dress, you begin to own and express your own perfect and intrinsic unlimited power.

CHAPTER 7

I see others as perfect powerful beings

One beautiful summer night in 1987, I left the Actor's Institute in New York City and headed home to Long Island. I passed by a homeless woman lying asleep in a doorway. I didn't have much cash with me, but I felt strongly that I should leave something anyway. I put some bills in the sleeping woman's hand and walked away. Then, I realized that I had depleted my cab fare and, in fact, only had enough money left to take the Long Island railroad. That meant a long, late night walk to Penn Station in four inch high heels.

After a few blocks and a developing blister, I decided to take off my shoes and walk barefoot the rest of the way. Since it was a warm, clear night it didn't seem like anything could stop me from enjoying the walk.

It had not yet occurred to me that the path I had chosen to walk to Penn Station would lead me through some less desirable areas. Just as I was passing by a burned out building, I noticed a large gang watching me from across the street. There was no one else around and the seriousness of the situation quickly became apparent. The gang crossed the street at an angle clearly intended to cut me off. I felt fear flow through me. My pulse quickened. Everything told me that this wasn't going to be good.

But then something shifted inside me. I remembered who they really were; intrinsically powerful beings playing the part of thugs because they had forgotten their own true power. The gang surrounded me matching my pace. I focused on the leader who had moved in and was walking beside me. Looking him straight in the eye; I smiled and said, "What a beautiful night – don't you think?" Dead silence. No response from anyone. The gang waited for a cue from him. No one made a sound for what seemed liked much longer than the few seconds it really was. I continued to walk, smiling up at him. Finally, the leader said "What's a good-lookin' girl like you doin' walking these streets alone? Don't you know how dangerous that is?" Then he insisted that he and his gang walk me all the way to Penn Station so that they could protect me.

By remembering my own intrinsic power and separating the behaviors of this gang from the intrinsically powerful beings I knew they really were; my potential attackers became my protectors – my enemies became my friends – and a potentially violent and destructive situation shifted into a positive empowering one for everyone involved.

As we recognize our inherent perfection and personal power, we are led to the natural conclusion that others are likewise amazing souls with equal inherent and intrinsic worth and power – even if, in the moment, they are acting otherwise. When we accept any environment into which we are led and pay attention to every soul within that environment; and when we treat them with respect and appreciation for who they really are; we create a larger space for possibilities of powerful positive connection even – especially – with the opposition. We help them recognize or at least feel their true power and make different choices even in the most unlikely of circumstances.

When others sense our acknowledgment and appreciation of who they really are and our comfortable connection with them, the results are amazing. Even in conflict or other apparently "adverse" circumstances, when we pay more attention to the people than to the conflict, productive and profitable relationships are often established with the "opposition."

What will happen to you in your relationships when you recognize not only your own, but other's intrinsic power and perfection? It only takes one person in a relationship to shift the relationship in profound ways. What would happen if that one person was you? How might you be able to shift even the worst relationship into one that supports everyone involved? You, and only you, have the power to create the kind of relationships you want and deserve.

CHAPTER 8

I often spontaneously sing out loud

Have you ever sent a singing pink gorilla to your spouse or a co-worker? It might have been me inside that pink fuzzy suit.

For years, I owned and operated a singing telegram service called "Sizzlegram." For the sheer joy of it, I sometimes went myself to offices and parties to sing the telegrams. The ironic part of this is that I can't sing. Actually I can sing – very badly!

For years, I believed that I was successful at singing the telegram messages because, let's face it, it doesn't matter how you sound when you are a pink gorilla. I realize now, however, that it wasn't my costume that made it work; it was because I was having so much fun that I created fun for everyone else. I showed up as "me" and didn't worry much about being embarrassed – after all, I was already pink!

When we are willing to risk a little "dignity" to express ourselves in fun, spontaneous ways, suddenly there is a bigger space for creative exploration and life becomes a joyous adventure.

It is in this state of play that great possibilities are often born. I recently conducted a seminar for a national company whose business started as a result of a random meeting on a ski lift at a mountain resort in Utah. They were having fun - possibly playing hooky from work - and certainly not looking to start a new company. It was in this space of fun and play that an ingenious new business was created and a down hill run became the ride of their lives.

When we let go of how we think we need to show up to get "respect"; when we let go of unnecessary and inappropriate self-imposed rules and expectations which don't support who we really are; when we let go of self censorship, laugh at our own blunders, and are willing to sing off key and out loud; we break out of limited perceptions and anything becomes possible.

This sense of play – so obvious in children – is still just below the surface in "dignified" adults; so when we embrace and encourage our sense of fun, we are also gently encouraging others to scrape off a layer or two and be a little closer to who they really are. We may at first feel scared or silly – our dignity threatened – to express our playful natures;

however, it is worth the attempt, because when one of us has the courage to "let it all hang out," it gives others permission to do the same – and in this expression of primal joy called "fun" we expose who we really are and for a moment at least, live in the fullness and richness of possibility.

Try it. Take the day off from being who you think you have to be. Go ahead. Have fun. What will that look like? What will you do? How will you do it? Then do it – and write to me and tell me what happens!

Nanice Ellis

CHAPTER 9

I effortlessly do what I say I will do

Our power is enhanced not only in following up our words with actions but also in choosing words and actions and making promises which support who we really are – our most powerful selves.

Does your "to do" list support who you are and the integrity of your personal and business life? What is missing from your list? Time with your family? Time to play? Time to create? Time for yourself? What would happen if you cleared the slate and started to rethink your life from the inside out? Would you then be able to do all the things you say you will do – with passion and enthusiasm?

When the things we say we will do reflect who we really are, actions effortlessly follow our words. We want to follow through with all we intend to do because it supports our highest vision of who we really are. Incongruence occurs when we allow ourselves to be manipulated into making commitments or respond out of feelings of guilt or obligation. This happens when we are not in touch with our own feelings and are not committed to who we truly know ourselves to be.

Can you uncover your truth without self judgment? Maybe this is your wake up call to finally get your life in order with your real self.

Many people allow themselves to be manipulated by friends, family (especially their children!), co-workers, and bosses – and they seem to survive just fine. But is that good enough - for you? Are you willing to settle for a life you get by looking good to everyone but yourself? Or are you looking to make a real difference and leave your part of the world better than you found it? Sure, even if you show up as less than who you are, you can still make a difference. There are many charities you can contribute to and organizations you can join to help others; but nothing makes as great a difference as simply being the powerful, creative, intuitively wise, generous being you will discover in yourself when you insist on being who you really are.

You have something to offer the world that only you can give. Perhaps it is your gifts or talents. It could be your understanding and compassion. It could simply be your way of seeing things that no one else can see. But whatever you give, your uniqueness brings something extraordinary to life. No one is better at being "you" than you. Your most important job is to be who you really are and adamantly and consistently support your real self with only those actions, behaviors and commitments that reflect who you really are.

This is your gift to the world. This is how you make a difference; being you – the real you. There are seven billion people in the world, but only one you. Of all the people who have ever lived and who will ever live, there is still only one you. You came here to discover and express who you really are. This is your most important job. The first thing on your "to do" list is just "to be" – you.

Others might at first resist your awakening. Those who are used to controlling and manipulating you will likely "turn up the heat". Life may get turned up side down. You will probably question your own decision to be yourself. But if you maintain the vision of who you are long enough for it to become a part of your fundamental beliefs, you will live an incredible life of joy and personal power which will reflect the greatest most powerful you.

Nanice Ellis

CHAPTER 10

I put people before profits

As a landlord, I had many unwanted opportunities to evict tenants. My initial instinct was to put the eviction notice on the door and run. This just did not feel right. It felt incongruous with who I was. So I decided to confront the very thing I was trying to avoid – the possibly angry or even tearful reaction of the tenant. One day, eviction notice in hand, I knocked on the door of a tenant who had repeatedly failed to pay his rent and was seriously in arrears. I handed him the notice of eviction saying, "You know I must give this to you, but would you tell me what's going on and how I can help?"

He invited me into his home. We sat down and talked like friends. His rent was needed in order to pay the mortgage. It was a business necessity that I had to evict him if he didn't pay the rent. But this wasn't just "business." This was an interaction with a wonderful intrinsically perfect being who was in a tough situation. I was absolutely certain of his value and my intent was to honor who he really was and his personal challenges which were hampering his ability to keep up with his financial obligations . During our hour long interaction, we connected above the level of tenant and landlord. When I got up to leave, he hugged me and thanked me. I had just evicted this man – and he thanked me! Shortly after our conversation he voluntarily left, making the adversarial and expensive legal process unnecessary.

Being responsible business people, we must make appropriate mutual commitments and set appropriate boundaries; however, that does not exclude us – or excuse us – from connecting at a higher level with those who might not like what we have to say or do at that moment. If we approach everyone with whom we do business with a clear knowing of their personal value and intrinsic power beyond their current circumstances, they will tend to honor and value who we are in return. And if we have to make a tough decision that they won't like, chances are that rather than turn on us with anger or resentment, they will gain a higher level of respect for us and for themselves and will appreciate us for treating them with respect and appreciation for the wonderful beings they really are.

Acknowledging and appreciating the value of others and "putting people before profits" does not weaken business; it enhances business because we lift ourselves, the person with whom we are dealing, and the business relationship to a higher level. We are more congruous and consistent – therefore more successful – in our business dealings as we better express who we really are and recognize the intrinsic value of others in the process of making a legitimate profit.

Nanice Ellis

CHAPTER 11

My identity is not attached to outcomes

When you succeed, how do you feel? Powerful? How do you feel when you fail? Powerless? Is it success or the lack of success which gives you your sense of power? Or is it your attachment to your idea or definition of success that changes how you feel about yourself? If we pass a test, we feel smart and powerful. If we get a promotion or raise, we feel established and worthy. If our kids get the best grades, we feel like wonderful parents. But when we fail the test – get fired – and our kids drop out of school – how do we feel then?

Things don't always work out the way we intend, no matter how much we plan. Sometimes life gets in the way of how we want to live. When that happens, most people feel tired, defeated, and powerless as they watch their goals and aspirations go down the drain.

When we consciously or unconsciously attach our sense of worth to "successful outcomes" we set ourselves to feel powerless most of the time. Things go wrong no matter how hard we try, so why should we attach our sense of personal worth and power to things we may not be able to control? Why can't we feel great and powerful even when we "fail"? We can - when we separate our sense of personal value and identity from that which can change (which is most everything). We then experience our worth as infinite and unchanging. We are valuable and powerful simply because we are. It is our natural state of being. We don't have to prove our worth – we need do nothing but accept the truth of our innate and infinite power.

Recently, hundreds of people lost their homes and possessions in a devastating Florida hurricane. Months before that many people lost their homes and possessions in fires that swept through the mountains in California. And even more recently hundreds of thousands lost everything in a devastating tidal wave. Are these people any less valuable after their losses than before? What about Christopher Reeves - Superman? Did he suddenly become worthless because he was no longer physically viable? Or was his worth, value and power beyond his physical capabilities?

When our sense of worth is dependent on external events, situations, or people, we do not consistently feel truly worthy. The very nature of life and living with its roller coaster ups and downs will always threaten the identity of those attached to outcomes. But what will happen when you accept that your worth and your power are not dependent on anyone or anything? When you separate external results from an internal knowing of who you really are, how will you approach life? You could risk everything because you would know that there was nothing at all to risk. You could win the lottery or lose it all.

No matter what the outcome, your powerful sense of self is absolute. No matter how much life changes for or against your plans – who you know yourself to be will remain constant and intact and you will feel consistently worthy and powerful – because you are – and the long term results of your life will reflect the intrinsically and inherently perfect and powerful being that you really are.

CHAPTER 12

*I do not compromise who
I am to get my needs met*

For years, I stayed in a relationship in the hopes that my needs for love, acceptance, and appreciation would be met. It wasn't happening. I believed that if I could somehow change, my significant other would see and hear me; and meet my needs.

What I did not understand was that as I was changing my outward behaviors and appearances – modifying and adjusting how I showed up in the relationship – in order to get these needs met, the person he was seeing and hearing was not "me." I had done an excellent job of compromising my real self in order to get something I thought was more important. It didn't work. I needed appreciation. I still wasn't getting it. Why? I was putting everything I had into it – wasn't I?

Finally one day as I asked that question for the thousandth time, I stopped; and quietly listened for the answer. And it came – silent, but clear. I thought I had put everything I had into this relationship, but I had left something very important out. Me. In my attempts to get love and appreciation I had sadly sacrificed the best of what I had to offer – the "real me".

What about you? Are you trying to get acceptance? Approval? Understanding? Love? The need to be seen, heard, or appreciated? These needs are valid, but are you giving up who you are in order to get them met? Is it working? Are you struggling to meet the expectations of others and still not feeling loved or valued? Are you holding back your truth for fear of confrontation? Are you concealing your ideas because someone might not agree? Are you putting everything you have into relationships except you – who you really are?

Are you playing small because your greatness might be threatening to another – your boss, your spouse, your significant other, your neighbors or your co-workers? When we change or diminish who we are in order to get others to accept us, it is not "us" they are accepting.

How can your needs be met if you sacrifice who you are in the process? Just as the need for food, water, or sleep tend to control our behavior until met; so will emotional needs for love, acceptance and appreciation etc…. It's important to get our needs met so that we are emotionally full and are then free to express our values.

"Needs" are what we require from the world to be safe, healthy, or complete. Values, on the other hand are what we want to give back. But we can't truly give without attachment (giving in order to get a need met in return) until we are full and overflowing ourselves. People who own their power can give abundantly because they make sure that their needs are met. They no longer manipulate or compromise their behavior in order to get others to meet their needs. They know that to own their power, they must first own their needs by understanding them, honoring them, and finding healthy and healing ways to meet their own needs rather than depend on others to meet them.

Ironically, if we don't give ourselves what we need, we can't even accept it from others even when it is given. Those who do not love themselves, cannot truly feel love from another; someone who does not appreciate their own worth, can hardly feel appreciated by someone else.

What would happen if we redirected the fulfillment of our needs to ourselves - if we let everyone else off the hook and stopped looking to others to give us what we really need to give to ourselves? How would you feel right now, if you unconditionally loved and accepted yourself? If you appreciated, understood, heard, and approved of yourself? You don't expect someone else to feed you or tuck you in bed at night, do you? So, why not be the owner and supplier of your emotional needs as well. You will still enjoy recognition and love and appreciation from others, but you won't need it (there is a big difference) when you fulfill your own needs.

So, how do you do that? How do you meet your own needs? How do you love and appreciate yourself? We have been told since forever that if we walk around telling ourselves how wonderful we are that we are egotistical, self centered, selfish, cocky, proud.... Do it anyway! Be your own best friend and cheerleader. Ask yourself, what would it look like if someone loved me (the way I want to be loved)? What would I want them to do? How would I want them to treat me? What would I want them to say to me? Say it to yourself; do it for yourself; and stop waiting for or depending on someone else's validation.

You can spend the rest of your life trying to get your needs met by people who may feel so empty they may have little to give to you. Every time you expect someone else to meet your needs, you divert your energy to them and ultimately you feel needy and powerless.

But what will happen in your relationships when you stop requiring or expecting others to meet your needs – especially needs they probably don't even know about? How will you show up at work, at home, in the marketplace, and at social events when you feel fully and happily accepted, loved, and appreciated, by the most important person in your life – you!

You don't need others to do something you can do for yourself. Take back your energy; know and express your power; own your own needs and meet them fully; thereby, enhancing your ability to step into your power and express it in the world. Accept and appreciate who you really are and honor that by giving to yourself the acceptance, love, and appreciation that as a perfect being you fully deserve. You will then be in position to contribute grandly and naturally to the world and ultimately live from your highest and greatest values as you consistently express who you really are and the mission you came here to fulfill.

Nanice Ellis

CHAPTER 13

*My thoughts and actions are not
influenced or controlled by others*

Do you sometimes withhold a thought or action because you are afraid of how others might respond? I don't mean are you sometimes careful in what you say in order to be polite or appropriate; I mean do you sometimes not express an honest opinion or desire because you feel you may lose the acceptance of others who are important to you – that you might lose your job, status, popularity, etc."

When we stop ourselves from sharing a thought or feeling that represents who we are because we are afraid of rejection or judgment, we compromise our power. Conversely, when we open up and appropriately but directly state the truth as we know it, we exercise our power.

We live powerfully when we accept, acknowledge, and are willing to express who we really are regardless of circumstances or consequences. Nothing you think you could possibly lose "out there" is more valuable than being who you really are "in here."

CHAPTER 14

I create the life I desire by living my own values regardless of consequences

Several years ago, one of my coaching clients was faced with a difficult choice. He had a great career with a big corporation in New York City. He was asked to tell a small lie – but one with huge implications – in order to protect a superior. It could have meant his job if he didn't. It would have been easy to say what he was being asked to say and difficult for anyone to find out. After days of consideration, he realized that even though this was only a small lie with minimal or no external consequences to him, it had huge internal consequences because it went against his own values. The internal consequence of not following his own inner voice – and being who he really was – was far greater than any external consequence that might follow his refusal to lie.

You may never have to make such a dramatic choice; but every day most of us ask ourselves or allow others to ask us to do things which go against who we are inside. It may be playing a role of caretaker, loner, life of the party, martyr, or victim, which no longer suits us and maybe never has. It could be working at a job that is contrary to our values or is so boring or restrictive that we count the minutes until we can go home, only to dread coming back the very next day. It could be waking up to someone who disrespects us or whose expectations outweigh who we want to be in the relationship or are otherwise contrary to who we are. That feeling of being emotionally, physically and spiritually diminished – often felt and treated as depression – may be the result of internal conflict resulting from trying to meet expectations and obligations that are not congruous with who we really are. We are not created to live according to expectations which drain our very being.

Conversely, we know that when our life is consistent with our values, we are energized and inspired to live the life we desire – and have consciously created for ourselves. Our deep personal values become our "inner guidance system," directing us to live according to who we really are.

How often do you make choices that are contrary to your true values and do not support who you are? Is it time to stop and ask yourself, "Is this important? To me? Really? Why? Who am I?

Who am I really?" Maybe it's time to sort through your values and determine if they are old hand-me-downs from your parents, church, or society; try them on, one at a time; and see if they fit who you are now or who you know yourself to be inside? If they don't, it is time to give them up.

What will happen when you rid yourself of old beliefs which push you to live some else's life by someone else's standards? What will happen when you go through your wardrobe of values and consciously choose to keep only those which support who you are and the life you desire? Can you imagine the extraordinary life you will create when you express your real self?

When we express who we really are, we are energized and inspired to create. Our actions are clear and focused and we naturally reveal our intrinsic power at every moment. We show up more consistent, enthused, effective, and loving in all areas of our lives. And we discover that what we have been looking for all along was simply being our own true selves.

Your greatest gift to yourself and the world is to be who you really are from this moment on.

Nanice Ellis

CHAPTER 15

I make peace a priority

For many years, I was a weary, overwhelmed real estate investor and landlord. My days consisted of "putting out fires" on properties I owned and was rehabilitating, dealing with tenant problems, juggling finances and in my spare time trying to find more properties to buy so I could continue the cycle! My life revolved around tenants calling me in the middle of the night with backed up toilets and getting financing on properties which should have been condemned – so that I could buy them and make them new again.

I finally had enough when, one Christmas Eve, the water heater went out at one of my apartment buildings. There was no one to call the night before Christmas so I tried to fix it myself. There I stood, in complete darkness, in knee deep stinky water in my best black dress and high heeled pumps, trying to get this ancient water heater to light so that my tenants would have hot water on Christmas. I never did get that old burner to light and had to knock on each tenant's door and inform them that they wouldn't be able to shower on Christmas morning or ever again until I could get someone to fix the old thing.

It suddenly occurred to me that I had become the "old thing" that needed fixing. I had allowed my idea of financial "success" to drag me off my higher path and drop me smack in the middle of turmoil. I'd had enough.

Because I had allowed myself to become invested in succeeding by the world's definition of the word instead of my own, I sacrificed my own well being for a financial outcome. I was so attached to this outcome that I had given up listening to my heart and soul which were silently screaming for peace. After many years, it became very clear that the thing I sought most was escaping me.

Why do we work so hard? Is it for security, luxury, success, status, or identity? Is it to live where and how we want to live? Or is it to obtain the feelings we assume the achievement of these goals will bring us? Happiness, love, connection, safety, security, approval, acceptance – peace?

My highest desire is for peace. But by chasing relentlessly after my material dreams, I kept pushing peace further and further away. The chase for what was "out there" was incongruous with the inner peace I was seeking. Finally, one day I realized my thoughts and actions had pushed peace completely out of my life. I was working so hard doing one thing to achieve another that I overlooked the fact that the "other" was there all along. In that moment of recognizing this truth, and by letting go of the idea that I had to achieve "success" in order to obtain "happiness" – I re-discovered peace.

I realized that peace could not be found through the attainment of, or attachment to, any person, place, or thing. In fact, peace is a natural result of being fully present in the moment and releasing any and all attachments.

Once I made peace a priority, I discovered that I could, in fact, experience peace in even the most undesirable circumstances. Even though I still gave up real estate as the primary source of my income, what I really gave up was my resistance to challenging experiences. It became clear to me that difficult experiences do not take peace away, but rather it is our mental approach to those challenges that distract us from peace.

And what is that distracting mental approach? It is our belief that the outcome makes us happy or unhappy; that the outcome makes us right or wrong; that the outcome determines whether we are successes or failures. It is our belief that outcomes determine who we are.

So how do you find peace? Simply this: release your attachment to outcomes. Stop judging yourself. Accept yourself and your circumstances just as they are now – without conditions. Know that you are born perfect and powerful and nothing you or anyone else does – no outcome, no result – can make you more or less than the perfect, powerful soul that you are and always have been.

Peace is not something that happens as a result of something else. Peace is a natural result of being who you really are and loving and accepting yourself regardless of outside circumstances. You don't have to do anything else. Ironically when you make peace a priority, you not only discover peace, you find that you are naturally inspired to take effective action when appropriate and you have more time, energy, and power with which to enjoy all the other things you sought in the first place – if you still desire them.

CHAPTER 16

I am the source of my own power

What is the source of your personal power? Money? Authority? Roles? Intelligence? Luck? Personal appearance and style? Of course you feel strong and powerful when you have the right relationships, strong finances, and good health (and good looks!); but how powerful do you really feel when your relationships stink, and you are sick and broke? How do you feel when you realize your power depends on external things which seem beyond your control?

I spent many years trying to establish and maintain my power through relationships, career, and money. But even when I felt accomplished in these areas, there remained nagging insecurity; the fear of loosing the things to which I attached my power. Because I believed my security and sense of self was dependent on my circumstances, I was in a constant state of anxious wariness, trying to preserve what I had by anticipating and controlling outside events which were beyond my control. The tension and energy drain was enormous.

I realized that no matter how strong I thought I was, I was not strong enough to keep pushing the heavy cart of circumstance laden with details up the steep hill of my life. The truth is, I often felt less powerful even as I achieved my desires because of the ever increasing fear and doubt that I could maintain what I had accomplished. Outside I appeared strong and successful, but inside I felt unhappy and drained of power.

One day, I realized that the only thing I had complete power over was my thoughts. At first that seemed insufficient, but soon I realized that was all that really mattered; because my thoughts – especially my understanding of who I really was – determined my sense of success. So I simply let go of the idea that outside events determined my power; and I took control of my own thoughts. I rejected the notion that power came from any outside person, thing or event. I focused on the universal truth that because my power is already intrinsic and inherently mine, no gain can give me power and no loss can strip me of it.

In a moment, I felt centered and balanced; unafraid of outside circumstances or consequences. For the first time in my life, I truly felt in control of my own destiny. No longer would my power be diffused by an endless quest of attaining and maintaining what I thought I needed in order to feel powerful. I accepted that the true source of my power is me – who I really am – an inherently and intrinsically perfect and powerful being. Almost instantly, the drain on my energy ceased, and my life filled with a calm awareness of my own unlimited power.

Victor Frankl was stripped of all his possessions – he lost his money, family, and basic human decencies – when imprisoned in a Nazi concentration camp. The thing that he could not be stripped of was his intrinsic and infinite power to know and internally honor himself – to choose how he would interpret and mentally approach his circumstances despite the loss of all to which he was previously attached.

What if you knew that the source of your power was you – who you really are? How will the way in which you live your life shift once you realize that your power is not attached to any thing outside yourself? How will it feel when you let go of the constant battle of achieving temporary success or status that could be taken away at any moment by events beyond your control?

What if the source of your own personal power was something that you could experience right this minute and every minute for the rest of your life and beyond – simply by understanding that the inherently perfectly powerful 'you' is now in control of your life?

There is only one thing we can always control and that is the way in which we think. Is the quality of our lives really contingent on outside events and circumstances? Or is it determined by "inside events" – how we communicate with ourselves, what we focus on, give our attention to, and believe?

What if searching for power through money, people and situations outside yourself actually distracts you from discovering and exercising your own inherent power? Is it possible that when you feel "lack" or "need" and feel you must look outside yourself for what you want; it is because you have forgotten that you are the source of your own power – and happiness?

External circumstances and conditions are not the source of your power – and never have been. Real power is inherently and intrinsically yours and can not be taken away. You can immediately experience success and security by remembering that you are the source of your own power -not external circumstances and conditions. Accept that, and you immediately begin to experience the results of your own constant and unlimited personal power.

CHAPTER 17

*I speak my mind and stand
up for my truth*

W hen she was only seventeen, I invited
April to live with me and my family in
our small three bedroom apartment. Her
mother had chosen to marry for the eighth time
and April was afraid of another, possibly abusive,
step father. I had personally experienced abuse
when I was her age and was deeply concerned.
April was my son's girlfriend and I had grown
to love her as my daughter. Inviting her into our
home permanently seemed like the only reasonable
solution under the circumstances.

April was shy and timid. She usually went
along with everything and rarely asked for anything.
Of course she had her own needs and opinions, but
she never spoke up because experience taught her
that speaking her mind could put her at serious
risk. As a child she survived by not challenging

authority. It "worked" because, despite abuse and neglect, she survived.

Now she was faced with a fresh choice (life often repeatedly offers us the same choice over and over again until we heal and embrace our power). She could shut down and go along with the decisions of her authority figures or she could stand up for herself and risk everything to gain her freedom. She took her first stand when she accepted our invitation to move in with us.

Her parents responded with anger. How could she reject her "family" and her strict religion and move in with her boyfriend's family after knowing them just a short time? Her natural father threatened me with legal action; he could do that, since his daughter was under age. I was quite willing to speak my mind in defense of April's decision – but I didn't. I remembered only too well my own history and I knew that if April would ever be free to express who she really was, the voice that needed expression was hers – not mine. I quietly held my tongue; hoping, believing, anticipating that April would reach within, take hold of her truth and voice it. And she did.

For the first time in her young life, April confronted her intimidating father. Though she was shaking inside, she told him clearly and calmly that she knew he could legally make her leave her chosen home; however, if he chose to do that, she would never live with him; rather she would live in foster care until she turned eighteen and her relationship with him would forever be alienated. On the other hand, if he was willing to respect her decision, even if he didn't like it, she was willing to create a new, healthier relationship built on a foundation of mutual respect and support. April found her voice and consequently discovered her power.

When we hold ourselves back, bite our tongues, stop expressing what we want and who we are out of fear, we divert our power to others – give it away in a sense; our actions become incongruous with who we really are and our personal power becomes scattered and defocused. But if we stand up and speak out, if we express our truths despite fear of the outcome, we may risk everything but we gain the knowing of our power.

You and only you know your truth; and only you have the power to live it. The first step in reclaiming your power is to be honest with yourself. Are you, right now, hiding in a life which doesn't support who you really are – completely? Don't judge yourself or your life but rather simply observe. How are you not being true to yourself in your relationships, your work, and all the other important areas of your life? Life is way too short to spend even one day denying your true feelings, making yourself small to continue a relationship, doing one thing in order to get another, and pushing your real self so far down that you end up living someone else's life on someone else's terms.

How might things have to change, what might you have to give up, what might confront you – if you expressed your truth? Are you concealing your truth because you are afraid of the consequences?

But what would happen if you expressed your truth without attachment to the outcome? What would happen to your fear of consequence? The truth is, every time you hide a part of you because you fear the consequences, you divert your power to the very thing you are afraid of.

It's time to wake up and start living your own life. Don't wait until you get so lost you don't know how to find yourself again. If you already feel lost, stop right now and make a commitment to yourself – your real self – that no matter what it takes, you will start telling the truth until you unravel that which you have called your life and reweave it into the life that suits who you really are – even if you don't have a clue what that looks like right now.

You are more powerful than anything or anyone you could possibly fear.

How much of your life have you given away to fear already? It is time to reclaim your life by reclaiming your power. If you wait even one more day, that will be one less day that you will experience the intrinsic life changing power of who you really are. It is time – now.

April has lived with us for over 7 years. She is my daughter as much as if she had been born to me. Her father has become a welcome part of our family as well.

Nanice Ellis

CHAPTER 18

I accept myself as I am —
unconditionally — right now

I t's easy to accept yourself when you do things "right" and everything is going great. But do you still accept yourself when circumstances aren't so great and you do something that is unacceptable to your friends, neighbors or co-workers? What if you do something that is unacceptable even to you? That is the acid test of unconditional self-acceptance.

I became a vegetarian at age 12 because I didn't believe in killing animals. I felt that all living things had a right to life. Even with the lure of eating delicious, steaming New York hot dogs, smothered in onions, from the corner vender with my friends did not sway me from my strong beliefs.

Then when I was 38, my house became infested with mice. I tried every natural remedy from sonic devices to herbal mists to get rid of them. Nothing worked. In fact, whatever I tried seemed to work as an aphrodisiac for the little critters. Months passed and my home became completely overrun with them.

You know you have a serious infestation of mice when you wake up in the middle of the night with one of those little guys running across your pillow; while his brother is leaving little "presents" for you on the kitchen counter. I had even stopped inviting people over to visit after a mouse ran across the foot of a horrified guest when we were having coffee in my living room. I had to do something. I had to do the "unacceptable." I went to Wal-Mart and bought mouse poison. It was one of the most difficult things I ever did. It went against one of my strongest beliefs. I did it anyway.

One day, I found one of their little carcasses. I felt so sad. But I also realized that, while I did not accept the act of killing, I still accepted myself – unconditionally. I had removed myself and who I knew I really was from my circumstantial decision and subsequent actions. I may have killed, but I was not a killer. I was still an intrinsically perfect being having a very difficult human experience.

No matter what you do or don't do; no matter who approves or doesn't approve; no matter what you believe you lost or threw away; you are still perfect and powerful. It's time to stop judging yourself. If you are waiting to be free of human imperfection in order to accept and realize your inherent perfection, forget it. It will never happen – not in this lifetime.

The very nature of our human experience requires us to be "imperfect." We are supposed to make mistakes. Life requires us to move out of our comfort zones and sometimes do things which others may not approve of – even do the things that we ourselves don't approve of – so that we can practice, learn and one day experience unconditional self acceptance despite our worst human expressions.

When you finally unconditionally accept your personal perfection regardless of your past or present actions and reactions or your roles and your relationships, what inner power will you experience? How will that enhance your ability to allow into your life what you truly desire? Judgment keeps us stuck in limiting beliefs and ineffective actions that are beneath our nobler selves. Unconditional self-acceptance frees us to attract, accept and experience the infinite possibilities of an abundant universe.

You are not your actions or reactions. You are not what you do or fail to do. You are an intrinsically perfect being who gets to have human misadventures – complete with mistakes that point out your apparent imperfection so you can discover and accept your intrinsic perfection.

Who would you be right now if you released all self judgment and accepted yourself unconditionally? How would you feel?

CHAPTER 19

*I am perfect and powerful
even when I "fail"*

My family and I decided to take a risk and venture into an alien environment filled with danger and adventure. We bought a boat. On our maiden voyage, my 21 year old son, Dustin promptly sank it – well, almost.

Immediately after launching, our beautiful new boat floundered and began to sink – fast! The natural laws governing buoyancy and air/water displacement showed no leniency as an icy cold stream of lake water shot into the boat's hold. I ran for help. While bemused strangers and a less than helpful park ranger watched, my son's girlfriend, April, desperately began to bail the water out using the largest receptacle she could find (a small Starbucks coffee cup). Dustin paced panicky on the shore speed-reading "Boating for Dummies" while Clay (5) and Travis (7) played on the sand, giving no consideration to the state of panic ensuing ten yards off shore. I ran from car to car *begging* for help. Everyone was so helpful, each simply asking, "Did you put the plug in?" I would scream that increasingly familiar question to Dustin and each time he would holler back an increasingly emphatic "Yes!" Finally someone said, "Did you put the plug in the *correct* hole?"

We dragged the sinking boat back onto the landing - discovering that Dustin did indeed put the plug in the wrong hole.

We are a relatively normal family, so of course we have never let Dustin live his faux pas down; but honestly, even as the boat was going under, I still saw my son as a brilliant, powerful soul. His potentially costly mistake had nothing to do with who he really was. Because I have always seen and treated my son as an intrinsically perfect soul empowered to take risks, he has learned to see himself the same way. He now shows up confidently in the business world as an artist – a creative graphic design genius (I am his mother and I say he is a genius) designing innovative websites and operating his own web hosting business. Genius that he is, I know that Dustin will never again put the boat plug in the wrong hole.

Life gives us plenty of opportunities to succeed and, it seems, even more opportunities to fail – and risk looking a little silly in the process. Working with thousands of people around the world through my workshops and personal coaching, I've learned that every one has a fear of failure in one sense or another. More particularly everyone seems to have a fear of being seen as a failure.

Even the most self assured CEO has a fear of being seen as a failure. What separates the successful leader from others is that desire and vision significantly out weigh the concern about failing. For many people, fear of failure keeps them from taking even reasonable chances. It's easier to live "safely" than to risk being seen as a failure.

You probably know how lousy it feels to fail – especially when others see it; but how great does it feel to succeed? To really succeed? To accomplish your grandest dream – your highest vision of the greatest you. What would that be like? What would you have to risk to get there?

You'd have to risk everything. You'd have to risk your image and identity in the world because you might not be able to maintain or regain it once you move out of your comfort zone.

You would also have to risk – nothing. You'd risk nothing because you'd realize that the greatest, most indestructible part of you could not be harmed or destroyed – you couldn't risk your identity or image because you would know that anything as limited or limiting as "identity and image" is not who you really are.

When we risk it all to live a dream or adventure, we soon discover that we actually risked nothing in order to discover everything.

You won't create the life you desire by giving into your fear of being seen as a failure and restricting yourself to doing the same limited things you've been doing. The world is waiting for you to play the part you came here to play – to risk expressing who you really are – to follow your heart and speak your mind – to be the greatest "you" the world has ever seen. This is your job – your only job.

Chapter 20

I let go of the energy scattering distractions of resentment and anger

Ⅰf you were to hear my mother talk about the woman who "did her wrong" 40 years ago, you would think it happened just yesterday. Why do we hang on to such grievances so long? Is it because we felt wronged, or because we still feel wronged?

Perhaps we feel we lost something because of what happened and still feel weakened or impoverished financially, emotionally, or physically. Maybe we lost a good job or money or even a spouse as a result of someone's thoughtlessness, interference, or abuse. It was unfair. It was! We were hurt. We feel a loss of power and react by hanging on to our grievance because we feel that we retain some control or power that we might lose if we let go.

Grievances and resentments should have a "sell by" date indicating that after a certain period of time the grievance should simple be discarded because it is outdated and not good for us. Because we are unconditionally powerful beings, no one can ever really hurt us in the first place – much less years after the act – and they certainly cannot actually take away our power. After all, if our power is intrinsic and inherent, we cannot lose it. But it can be misdirected and spent on old memories or turned inward in depression or anger.

Dwelling on past "wrongs," which no longer even exist in the real world, wastes our attention and power on things that are past – gone – non-existent – toast. Powerful people simply don't have the time or interest in dwelling on the past.

Every day that we hang on to an outdated grievance, we spend our energy in our "death grip" on the grievance and rob ourselves of our ability to use our personal power more constructively. For every grudge we hang on to because we choose not to forgive and release, we divert, scatter, misdirect, or mis-express our energy and power.

Powerful people – that is to say, people who express their inherent power in constructive ways – are more interested in experiencing their power in the present – in every situation – including (and especially) difficult situations which seem disappointing or hurtful. They understand that the experience of power is available to all of us at any given moment simply by shifting our focus to that which supports the inherent infinite power and intrinsic perfection of who we really are – and doesn't distract us from our path. If you really are an intrinsically powerful being, how can anyone or anything compromise or take away your power? We only hold grudges when we buy into the illusion that someone has actually harmed us; and that our power is contingent on how the world treats us.

You can only hold a grudge if you forget how truly perfect, powerful, and therefore invincible you really are. But if you are determined to do so, please first consider how much work it takes. It is very energy-draining. To hold a grudge, we must first suppress the knowledge that we are infinitely and intrinsically powerful. Then we must forget our intrinsic perfection. Then we must forget that no one really can hurt an eternal soul. Then we have to remember all the details of the injury or slight. Then we must keep going over and over and over and over the problem or situation just to keep it fresh….

Need I say more? How much easier is it to simply remember the situation just enough to avoid (wherever possible) a similar situation in the future; focus on who we really are and the intrinsic perfection and power we inherently possess, and use our power to move forward.

Next time someone "does you wrong," remember that your experience of personal power starts and ends in your mind. No matter what happens, it is your interpretation of it and how you process the experience which allows you to feel powerless or powerful. If this is hard for you, if you really believe they took something from you, then try this: Give it back to yourself. Did they take love away? Love yourself and let love come to you. Did they take respect away, understand who you really are and respect yourself. Did they take security away? Find security in the knowledge that you are a perfect and powerful soul and nothing can harm you in any significant way. You are already perfect – you are already powerful – there is nothing outside of you that you need to complete your perfection or enhance your power. You need only remember the truth of your being.

You have the choice to keep giving power to the areas of your life you feel powerless - even if it is the past- or you can take responsibility for all your experiences and finally know the power of who you really are. It is time to re-focus your power. Know that your power is already unconditional and unlimited - the experience of your power is the direct result of your choice. Resolve the wrongs of the past and remove their power in the present. Let go of the resentment that results from your feeling that you are still experiencing harm or loss.

Know that nothing has ever nor can ever harm you. Choose new thoughts and interpretations about situations, persons or experiences, past or present. See them as challenges to overcome, experiences to enjoy, opportunities to learn – and accept them with gratitude as gifts from a Divine source…

…and suddenly your power is present and focused. You no longer feel the need to do anything to be powerful. You know that nothing and no one can diminish or take away your power. Know that you have everything you need right this second to know and experience your true and unabridged power. Feel the power in and through you – right now – and enjoy your most perfect and powerful life.

Nanice Ellis

CHAPTER 21

Faith guides me to express my real self

L ife seemed good. I was healthy and active; lived in a beautiful home with my 3 fantastic sons; had a long term relationship; and was building a successful business as a real estate investor. I was doing very well by anyone's standards – except mine.

Somewhere in the "worldly" equation of success, I felt that I had sold out who I really was in my pursuit of things I thought I needed to "survive" and be happy.

I had always dreamed of going to Paris, and so I did. One beautiful evening, I was standing atop the Eiffel tower, in the city of love, the place where dreams are created, gazing out over the sparkling city below. I thought, "This is nice."

NICE? This is NICE? A lifelong dream and it is nice? I had looked forward to this trip for years – and now I didn't really even care that I was there. I stood there, tears welling in my eyes. Something was missing. I felt as if I had left something behind

– something important. Then I got it. On my journey to success and happiness, I had left me behind.

I had to go "back". I had to find the part of me I left behind. I had to re-assess my journey, re-examine my life, and make sure that my future plans and progress – my journey of life – included me – who I really was. Before I could continue my worldly journey, I had to complete a different quest. I had to discover who I really was.

It would take me many months to assess each part of my life and decide what supported who I really was and what did not. I had to decide what was important to me – and firmly, make some tough decisions. It would take a lot of strength to let go of the parts of my life which didn't support my real self, but I knew it was critically important for me to get clear on the itinerary for the real journey I was meant to take so that I never left me behind again.

I realized that somewhere on the way to creating the life I had, I sacrificed my power by letting go of my greatest dreams. This wasn't about blame. I was a responsible, loving single mom. I honestly thought I had to turn away from my personal, more altruistic, aspirations in order to "get real" and support myself and my family. I didn't believe that the life which called me could support me. Now I realized the life I had created by being "practical" and "self sacrificing" didn't support me or my mission; and by not being true to who I really was, I wasn't supporting my family in deeper ways.

In the long run, my self sacrifice served no one. By not showing up as my real self, I deprived my family, friends, and business associates of the benefit of being with a fully realized soul showing up as who I really am.

It was time for me to let go of everything which did not support the real me – and cost so much needless time and attention. It was time to dedicate my real self to the purpose and message I came to this planet to share. But what if I had to lose all my worldly possessions – my very identity in the professional world – in order to re-discover and show up as my real self? Even that sacrifice would be small in comparison to the power and passion I would gain.

Like a fledgling eagle, I teetered on the edge of the cliff looking into a bottomless void. I was afraid; but faith, and the undeniable need to express who I really am, pulled me over. In one fell swoop I ended my long term relationship and my career as a real estate investor.

Taking that first leap of faith was all I needed to do. Right? Wrong! The winds of fear swept up and engulfed me. I found myself in huge financial challenges; I faced foreclosure, repossession and bankruptcy. This was terrifying. But it wasn't too late. I could still turn back. Maybe I had jumped too soon. What if I really couldn't fly? I had no parachute to break my fall. This was pretty extreme. Maybe I wasn't ready. My children deserved security. I could do this later. It seemed the prudent thing to do. I could turn back to safety…

…but at what cost? Should I give up my life – even to save my life? Again and again the choice presented itself. But despite the dizzying fear of falling, by taking the leap of faith and expressing who I really was, I felt alive. I was finally free.

And it was so good to feel free and alive again. It was suddenly very clear to me that you can't discover your power living someone else's life. Knowing your intrinsic power can only come from knowing and expressing your real self.

So I knew I must stay on course (even if was straight down!) because it was the flight path of faith that my inner guiding voice – the voice of who I really am – insisted I take. I continued to focus with clear intent on who I was and what I needed to do to express my real self. I aligned all my resources - personal, financial, spiritual - with the direction my leap of faith was taking me. I refused to give any strength to the fear screaming in my chest. I was committed to my purpose and held firm to my vision. I would do what I needed to do regardless of the outcome. I stayed the course.

Then, just as it seemed that I would crash, I caught the updraft – or it caught me. My clear commitment to myself, my purpose and the infinite possibilities of my life began to attract exactly what I needed just when I needed it. In the nick of time – usually in ways that I could not have planned – ways I never would have thought of or created by myself – the universe sustained me. Opportunities, new friends, and business colleagues appeared as if out of nowhere and became "the wind beneath my wings." Being who I really am attracted exactly who and what I needed – when I needed it – and soon I was living the life I really wanted - and wanted me.

Like you, sometimes life is a real challenge for me; but nothing like the inner struggle of standing on the Eiffel tower thinking this is "nice" and wondering why my journey felt so meaningless. Now I move in faith that being who I am will bring me all I need. And it does. I have never been happier

Are you being who you really are? Does your journey in life support "you"? What will it look like when you decide to move in faith and live the life you came here to live? What will happen when you let faith, which moves you forward, grow stronger than fear which holds you back? It might only mean finding some quiet time for yourself every day. Time to exercise, or to think, or meditate; or write that book you have wanted to write, or take a new class. It might also mean letting go of the professional and social – even religious – identity to which you are attached.

Whatever it is, isn't it time to find out for sure? This quest to rediscover who you really are so that your journey through life will be meaningful and joyful, requires an unconditionally trustworthy companion. Faith.

I am not asking you to do anything extreme, unless you know that is what you must do. Acting on faith is not jumping out of a plane without a parachute or setting sail in a leaky boat. Acting on faith comes from knowing yourself: what makes you happy, what makes you sad, what makes you – you; and then having the courage to act on who you really are with positive and powerful actions. Faith comes from choosing between your real self and the "you" that you somehow became on the "road to success." Faith is knowing that no matter what fear presents – even the fear of failing – you will still be fine because you are an intrinsically and inherently perfect powerful being. Nothing can really harm you.

No matter who you are or how successful your journey of life may seem, no journey is meaningful if you leave "you" behind. The quest before the journey is to discover your real self and create a life map which takes you along and supports your greatest vision of who you really are.

Nanice Ellis

CHAPTER 22

I allow myself to feel fear
— and move through it

I felt as if I were driving to my own funeral. In just under an hour, I would be jumping out of a plane for the first time. I had wanted to skydive since I was fourteen. My mother told me that as soon as I turned 18, I could do whatever I wanted. Each birthday was a year closer to my dream of being free to do as I pleased.

On my eighteenth birthday, I was ready and willing, but not able. I was 8 months pregnant (when they talk about tandem jumping, this is not what they have in mind). Without any feelings of loss or regret, I set my dream aside for a time. As I got older, the dream faded; but still remained a distant possibility. Now, over two decades later, here I was; headed to the airport with my now 23 year old son – on his birthday. We would toss our fates to the winds – quite literally – and face fear together. It was worth the wait.

There's not much training when you take your first jump. You're attached to a tandem master and (they assure you) there is not much that can go wrong. Of course they then hand you the long injury/death disclaimer to sign. (If anyone ever read it in detail, I'm sure they'd get right back in their car and never think of jumping out of a plane again.)

They prepared us for the jump by tightly harnessing us, and leading us to the plane. Anyway, I think it was a plane; it was a small metal box with what appeared to be wings. It looked and sounded like it was under construction. We had to sit on the floor facing the back of the plane – execution style – with our tandem masters sitting snugly behind us. If I had any doubts I would make the jump, it was canceled by the fact that landing in this wannabe plane was much more frightening than jumping out of it. It didn't help calm my nerves to see that the pilot already had his own parachute on!

It took thirty minutes to approach the drop zone. During that time my extreme fear melted into a curious calmness. Because I allowed myself to feel my feelings completely without judgment or resistance, they faded into this calm knowing. I knew that I would make this jump. I knew that the parachute would open. I knew that I would never again be the same.

When the pilot yelled "door", the door of the plane swung open furiously. Immediately 120 mile an hour winds engulfed us in shock. It was ten times worse than anything we could have anticipated. We were literally slapped in the face by the winds of reality. Fear returned with a fury.

Dustin and his tandem master exited the plane first. Now, I not only feared for me I feared for him. Seconds later, my tandem master ordered me to step out onto the wing strut – yes, that's right – to exit this plane, I had to step into space facing the back of the plane with hurricane force wind sucking the breath out of me; and *carefully* place my feet on a piece of vibrating metal no wider than my cell phone – and do this with my arms crossed!

I will never forget my feelings of power, powerlessness, freedom, exhilaration, fear, panic, anticipation, and resignation to my fate as I looked down and out and away – and seeing nothing but endless skies and small specs 12,000 feet below. Was I crazy? What was I doing? With no time to answer these questions, my tandem master yelled "GO".

As I learned in training, this meant I was to do 3 things: (1) look upward, (2) arch my back and (3) bend my legs towards my posterior. Well, I managed to do two of the three things. They say "Two out of three ain't bad." Well, they are wrong. Suddenly, we were falling head over heals – tumbling rapidly through the air – fear, like I had never known before, pulsed through me. When we finally stopped, I was facing upward. I never did this before, but I knew I wasn't supposed to be facing the sky! A quick motion from my tandem master, and we flipped over facing the earth as we should have been. At that moment, I realized I had entrusted my life to a man – cinched tightly to my back – someone I had not even known an hour before.

I've been told that skydiving feels like flying; but for me it felt like falling! Because I WAS falling, falling, falling fast to the rapidly approaching, very hard ground. I never got past the fear to really enjoy the experience. By the time we landed, I was in shock and stayed in a state of shock for hours, perhaps days.

I have never experienced fear as I did that day. The curious thing is that I knew beyond doubt that the parachute would open and I would walk away unharmed. So, why then was I fearful? If I wasn't afraid of dying or being seriously injured, what then was the source of my fear?

When you ask people about their fears and what they would do if the thing they feared actually happened, they will most likely tell you that they really don't believe that outcome will happen; or even if it does, they know they will be fine. So, if they are really not afraid of the outcome, what is there to fear? What then are they really afraid of?

What we are really afraid of is how we will feel by the envisioned experience. We're not afraid of what will actually happen as much as we are afraid of how it will make us feel. Ironically, every time we fear the thing we anticipate, we are actually feeling the way we are afraid to feel. Our fear creates exactly what we are afraid of; a dreaded undesirable feeling. What we are trying to avoid, we create.

What would happen if you changed your visualization; if you changed the idea of what could happen in your mind? Isn't this the only place this experience and your fear exist anyway? Fear is an emotional reaction designed to keep you from doing anything which threatens your physical life or your identity. And it does a great job. It will keep you safe and small if you allow it to dictate what you do and how you do it. I'm not suggesting you go skydiving, but what would happen if you remembered your inherent power while experiencing or imagining a threatening or frightening situation? How might you start living your life? What would you ask for and how would you show up? What impossibilities would suddenly become possible?

It is possible to live fearlessly when you know that your highest identity is not attached to anything or anyone. The fear that may now block your vision and your path becomes inconsequential in the choices you make. There is someone strapped to your back – protecting you from failing and falling. This someone is not your father, mother, teacher, friend, minister or tandem master– or even guardian angel; this someone is YOU. The eternal knowing of who you really are, the infinitely powerful you; immune from harm no matter what happens.

You are the Answer to Every Question You have ever Asked...

Unlimited power resonates within you right now - ready and available to be expressed in every area of your life. Nothing can diminish your inherent perfection and nothing can stop you from expressing your abundant power.

It may seem as if negative experiences hold us back and keep us from expressing our power but nothing can be further from the truth. These so called negative experiences that we think invalidate or harm us – give us opportunities to experience our courage and move us to release the power which is constant within us.

Think of the times in your life when you felt most powerful. When you overcame an obstacle or challenge or passed a difficult test. When you finished a project that seemed beyond your capabilities, triumphed over a physical or emotional disability, or faced a fear and moved beyond it. When you communicated your truth when you really wanted to run away; or simply were yourself when it would have been safer to hide. These are the times when you initially felt most weak and vulnerable – even hurt or ashamed. These are also your most powerful moments; because without such discomfort and fear, your power would never have been manifest. These challenges that occur in our lives are eternal gifts that give us the opportunity to reach deep within ourselves and find strength and courage we otherwise didn't know we possessed. These moments give you the opportunity to experience the infinite power which right now lies within you.

Does this mean that we have to wait for a challenge to experience our true power? No. It is ready to be expressed now. A "challenge" does not need to occur in order for our power to be manifest unless we insist by continuously diminishing and disbelieving in ourselves and our power.

Whatever personal power you have experienced in your life, your true infinite power is so much greater than anything you have yet known. The more experiences of power we have and the longer we are able to "sit in our power", the greater the knowing of what is truly possible.

Power lies in the infinite knowing of the intrinsic perfection of who you really are. It is expressed when you have the courage to be yourself – to be different – to express what others seem to hide. It expresses itself in your courage to be vulnerable and is honored as you accept responsibility for every thought, feeling and action. It is manifest in the ability to laugh at yourself and to learn from every experience and interaction; taking risks and living life to the fullest (knowing that there is really nothing to risk).

Your personal perfection is honored when you release ALL blame and self judgment for so-called mistakes. It is magnified when you accept that no one and nothing can ever take away or diminish your power. It is enhanced as you create a life which reflects who you really are.

Your power and perfection are evidenced as you act with such faith in the divine guidance that runs through you, that you can finally let go of the need to control anything. It results in your cup overflowing with such abundance that you give effortlessly and constantly to others without a thought of running out. You tap the infinite well of possibility knowing that you really can create anything you desire – simply because you desire it. You know that you are connected with every other soul – that you are all one and only one. And as you express who you really are, you create a larger space for others to express who they really are as well.

Knowing your infinite power begins with unconditionally respecting, honoring, accepting and loving the infinite beauty and intelligence that is you – even if the external world is currently saying otherwise. The time to do that is now.

Until the day you choose to completely know who you really are and experience and express the perfection and power within you, I will hold the space and vision for your greatest most powerful self because I know and see the Infinite Power of You!

Nanice Ellis

If you knew you possessed infinite and intrinsic power, right now, who would you be?

_____

_____

_____

_____

How would you feel?

_____

_____

_____

_____

_____

What would you have to give up in order to express that perfect and powerful being?

_____

_____

_____

_____

What limiting beliefs would have to be released?

_____

_____

_____

_____

_____

What truth would need expression?

_____

_____

_____

_____

_____

What fear would easily be overcome?

_____

_____

_____

_____

_____

What dream would be taken hold of?

_____

_____

_____

_____

Nanice Ellis

About Nanice

Often described as "a breath of fresh air," Nanice Ellis knows how to light your way through the place you're most afraid of, and gently guide you to the other side of your most personal darkness. Having made this journey herself as a survivor of a near-deadly abusive relationship, she challenges listeners: What would life be like if you actually unconditionally loved yourself? She explains why this is both the essential first step in spirituality AND the key to healing the world's ills.

As host of Chai with Nanice, international personal and corporate coach, author, master intuitive and keynote speaker, Nanice is a synthesizer who provides the safety to become fear-free to those who sincerely want to "be the change" they want to see.

The Infinite Power of You!

Nanice Ellis

Radio Talk Show Host of "Chai with Nanice",
Spiritual Guide, Speaker and Author of

- The Infinite Power of You!
- Even Gandhi Got Hungry and Buddha Got Mad!
- ZestPoint
- LipPrints
- What if...
- The Gratitude Journal
- Out of The Jungle

Nanice is available for Workshops, Presentations and Keynotes, as well as Tele-conferencing and One-on-One Coaching sessions.

Visit www.Nanice.com podcasts, insightful articles, life enhancement quizzes, free downloads and to order more books!

Nanice Ellis

www.Nanice.com
Nanice@Nanice.com

71642473R00068

Made in the USA
Middletown, DE
26 April 2018